MARILYN MONROE

MARILYN MONROE

A Life in Pictures

Edited by Anne Verlhac

Foreword by David Thomson

CHRONICLE BOOKS

SAN FRANCISCO

MARILYN MONROE: THE MOMENT AND OUR MEMORY

By David Thomson

"Marilyn Monroe" is legendary, her icon a smiling postage stamp for the ages. That was what Andy Warhol saw in the logo of her famous grin—brave, teasing, and beyond meaning. When we use her name now we mean so many things on which she has no comment: that she was a slave in a male society; that she was a harbinger of feminist awareness; that she was a talent crushed by her industry; or that she was not too talented, but raised to a point of terrible, maximum output by her business. What can we be sure of?

There is always the police report language, even if we live in a culture that may prefer to trust novelists who never met her. By that tough police standard, Norma Jeane Mortenson easily seems like human wreckage. She was born in Los Angeles on June 1, 1926, the child of Gladys Pearl Baker. On her birth certificate, the father was said to be Edward Mortenson, a baker. He was killed in a motorcycle accident when Norma Jeane was three years old. But it's unlikely he was her real father, and she probably never knew who her father was. The novelist loves this, for it encourages him to see a helpless, questioning gaze in those infant eyes. He imagines a life of futile quest, and he falls back on the oldest cliché from psychotherapy—everyone deserves a Daddy.

Or a Mommy. Either one. The police account has to admit that Gladys was unstable. For part of Norma Jeane's childhood, her mother was confined in public mental institutions back when they would have been frightening places. During those times, Norma Jeane was put in foster homes (as a state charge in an age that had no funding provision for indigent orphans). Norma Jeane said she was abused and raped in those places. Some say she made up those stories. She was "imaginative," but when she tried out for a school play she failed to get a part. In her childhood photographs, she has a winning smile—but is that her or the pressure of the orphanage, or an early instinct about photography? Norma spent her early teens with a friend of her mother. She quit high school at age sixteen, without graduating. So she got married—to Jim Dougherty, aged twenty-one, an aircraft factory worker—for the best reason: to get out of foster homes.

The envelope with the police report spills out a couple dozen photographs that chart her progress through age sixteen and married life. Why not? In the twentieth century, everyone was photographed.

Indeed, the camera is the only way of keeping up with an amazing explosion of population. Without photographs, every "one" is just a card in an endless file. And the photograph offers something else— we can't say it's the immediate, complete revelation of "soul" or "personality," but as bored fingers sort through all the pix, there can be a hesitation (at least) and a murmured, "Hey, baby!" as some stranger sees her wary smile at the lens, like Bambi waiting to see if she becomes a pet—or pet food. Some people photograph in ways that halt the automatic survey.

Norma Jeane's marriage to Jim Dougherty lasted from 1942 until 1944, when he left to join the Merchant Marine. Was this a normal life, or something like it, living in a bungalow in Van Nuys? Playing the cute wife to an athletic-looking guy? But there were no children, or pregnancies, or so it seems. She never says that Jim was anything other than a kind husband, one she called "Daddy." And he remains fond of her, at the same time admitting that her cooking was limited. He also tells an intriguing story. One day, they were out riding horses together—California was so much more open then. Dusk falls, but the horses plod on.

"How do they see in the dark?" Norma wants to know.

Jim replies with a wisecrack. "Just turn on the headlights," he says.

And then Norma Jeane does this wondrous thing. In the twilight, she looks her horse up and down, searching for a switch, and she says, "Where are they?" Jim never worked out whether she is truly dumb or just awfully cute pretending to be. But it is a habit, or a trick, that she will use a lot. It is a way of passing in a world where she is scared of being humiliated: if she makes a mistake, she meant to—she was being a dumb blonde.

How does an untrained natural work that out without being in front of a mirror for hours at a time, practicing her different looks? It's like working on a muscle, so that those who understand the muscle will notice it. Already, Norma Jeane is being noticed by camera people. Guys ask if they can photograph her. Evidence suggests studs, sometimes with no film in their cameras but horniness in their hearts, plus a few gay guys, shy boys, camera artists—people who see some vulnerability in her. She does pin-ups for the armed forces, beach shots. Her brown-red hair goes blonde.

There is the famous shot of her on ruffled red silk, stretched out, southwest to northeast, her long curled hair red, her body without an ounce of fat, her breasts with large brown nipples, her head tossed back so she can keep an eye on the cameraman. It's a shot from the late 1940s, so no pubic hair, not a truly dirty thought in sight. The story goes that Marilyn got very frightened when she thought this picture might stop her career. But that's just smarts acting dumb. The picture was as deliberate as any step in a professional career. It wouldn't be a surprise to learn that Johnny Hyde—her first valuable friend—was at the cameraman's shoulder, directing the entire thing.

More than that picture was the line that would go with it. When asked about the picture, reporters tossed in this question, "And you had nothing on?"

"Oh, I had the radio on," she replies—it brings the house down, and then she gives the guys that surprised look, as if to ask, "Did I say something funny?" It's a routine she likes. She runs the same joke later on, when all she has on is Chanel No. 5 instead of the radio. By the late '40s, she had a sure sense of what she wanted to be: something in the movies. When she posed for Tom Kelly for that red silk calendar picture, she got $50 and she signed the release form "Mona Monroe"—it's not a bad name for a B picture doll, but "Marilyn Monroe" (her movie name) has got so much more rhythm. So she was thinking about those things—and she was very far from an unknown. She was being talked about.

She made a few films in 1948, doing not very much except pushing her open-mouthed smile in front of the lens and hoping to be noticed. There's a group shot of eight girls from 20th Century-Fox Film Corporation, taken in 1950. Only three of the eight look at the camera, as if to say, "Hey, it's me." Only two have their mouths open. Only one is bright blonde. Marilyn is one, two, and three.

The director George Cukor saw her, and he noticed her tricks: "She had this absolute, unerring touch with comedy. In real life she didn't seem funny, but she had this touch. She acted as if she didn't quite understand why it was funny, which is what made it so funny … In certain ways she was very shrewd. I once heard her talk in her ordinary voice, which was quite unattractive. So she invented this appealing baby voice. Also, you very seldom saw her with her mouth closed, because when it was closed she had a very determined chin, almost a different face."

We would need to be very naive to believe that the "appealing baby voice" was all she had. Marilyn was making her way in the old Hollywood. John Huston remembered noticing her in 1949, "a very pretty girl, young and appealing, but so are thousands of girls in Hollywood." He fancied that she was casting-couch material—available for anyone who'd give her a screen test. So he passed on her. But then the agent, Johnny Hyde, appeared with her, and that's how she got the role of Angela in *The Asphalt Jungle*, a lovely little cameo, a perfect attention-getter, where she was a "baby" with a woman's body.

Hyde, a married man, old enough to be her grandfather, was dying. He had a bad heart, and Marilyn tried to make love gently to him until he told her it wasn't the gentleness he was seeking. She called him Daddy, too, and she earned the hatred of the Hyde family. She told the story of how, when Hyde died, she got into the morgue and laid beside his naked body trying to tell his ghost how much she had cared for him.

Not long after Hyde's death, she met Elia Kazan, the hottest director of stage and film, and a very good man to meet. He listened to her, he got her to talk about herself. He had learned that no other method was as seductive with young actresses in Hollywood. The only thing they wanted was respect. She told Kazan that there had been another man, "Fred," a musician. "He said she was no good for anything except fucking. He found her dress 'cheap.' He told her her breasts were too big. He didn't like to sleep in the same bed with her." And when he abused her, she came. Kazan thought she was honest, and touching, but "there was a fatal contradiction in Marilyn. She deeply wanted reassurance of her worth. Yet she respected the men who scorned her, because their estimate of her was her own."

Kazan said that he and Marilyn had great sex—"She had a bomb inside her. Ignite her and she exploded."—but men are likely to see their own accomplishment as a kind of fireworks. Others said Monroe was sedate, reserved, and worried about her own body. Perhaps the truth is that she was different with different men, because she noticed the differences and knew that in Hollywood she was a piece of meat, expected to look wide-eyed when the guys made dirty jokes about her.

In a way, she kept getting discovered: first she was Johnny Hyde's girl; then Kazan was looking after her; then John Huston gave her a cameo; and there was another eye-catching small role, for Joseph L. Mankiewicz in *All About Eve*, where she was the one woman in the picture who plainly had no talent as an actress—she was Miss Caswell, of the Copacabana School of Dramatic Art (in other words, she was a joke in a film about women who could talk, scheme, and make their way).

But Huston didn't use her again (or not until *The Misfits*, in a different age), Mankiewicz cast her just the once, and Kazan—the best director of actors she knew—never used her. It's hard not to look at these facts without picking up on industry wisdom: yes, she was a knockout in the right scenes or poses, and funny in her little-girl way, but could she play a developing character or say real lines? Or did you have to serve her up with small, piquant situations and half-lines of dialogue that were hers alone? Was Marilyn Monroe going to be an actress, or a photographed phenomenon—a tribute to the moment?

In the early 1950s, she made a string of pictures that hardly anyone has heard of despite her fame: *The Fireball*, *Right Cross*, *Home Town Story*, *As Young As You Feel*, *Love Nest*, *Let's Make It Legal*, *We're Not Married*. She was going nowhere again at a time when great screen careers were starting. Just as Marilyn struggled to be more than a pinup, people like Audrey Hepburn, Grace Kelly, Judy Holliday, and Ava Gardner were coming into being, along with someone named Elizabeth Taylor. They looked cool, classy, superior. They were women with brains, though Judy Holliday scooped up the Oscar doing a classic "dumb blonde" part. Everyone knew that Holliday was a very smart actress. They still thought Marilyn was searching for the headlights. No one—not even Marilyn—believed she had a ghost of a chance playing long, complex dialogue scenes, like those in *Born Yesterday*.

So she had to be discovered again. The great German director Fritz Lang put her in *Clash by Night* and he thought she had a freshness—but how much freshness does a woman need? Lang also despaired over her being late and not remembering her lines. Worse still, she wanted a drama coach on set with her to instruct her! Barbara Stanwyck, a great old pro, who likely recalled every line she'd ever spoken in movies, was in the same film. But Marilyn had amazing trouble putting words together. No one paused to notice she'd had no education.

And then, one of Hollywood's great discoverers, Howard Hawks, put her in two films that made her famous—*Monkey Business* and *Gentlemen Prefer Blondes*. In the first she played a secretary in a laboratory doing experiments on rejuvenation: every actor in sight, and the monkeys, were after her. She was funny, because of the situation and that wide-eyed look. The film was a dirty joke winking behind her back. But in *Gentlemen Prefer Blondes*, she was Lorelei Lee, the greatest blonde in American culture.

She sang—"Diamonds Are a Girl's Best Friend"—and she loved to sing. Suddenly the words flowed (though Marni Nixon had to dub in a few tricky lines). She wore great gowns. She had scenes with dirty old men and grave little boys, and Jane Russell was such a good pal. Marilyn looked confident for the first time, but Hawks had seen the truth: "She was the most frightened little girl. There wasn't a real thing about her. They tried to make her play real parts in a couple of pictures, and the pictures were disasters."

This was the great moment of Marilyn being "Marilyn," when her pinup reputation really coincided with some on-screen performances. In January 1954, she married Joe DiMaggio, who was just retiring from a great baseball career with the New York Yankees. Under his influence, she became a New York girl, not just a Californian babe. It seemed to a foolish public like a marriage made in heaven. In truth, it was hell: DiMaggio was Italian, conservative, and grim-minded. He had just retired, and when athletes retire they hit depression. Marilyn was becoming more famous every minute. Her crowds dwarfed his. He sulked. She stood on the streets of New York, over a subway grating, and went ecstatic when the draft lifted up her white dress and showed her panties. She was filming *The Seven Year Itch* for Billy Wilder and it was as good as it would get. The film was a big hit (and a constant dirty joke). DiMaggio began to leave her. Being in New York had fixed her allegiance to the Actors Studio. She was going to classes, worshipping at the feet of guru Lee Strasberg, confiding in Lee's homely wife Paula (the drama coach), and being friends with their daughter, Susan. Lee Strasberg said he thought she might be a great actress in hiding— if only the world would give her a chance. She studied parts, and there are legends of great improvs or half-performances at the Studio. There was talk of her doing Dostoyevsky or Chekhov. It never happened, except in her dreams. Not all the Strasbergs together could teach her to learn lines.

And, as a Fox contract player, she got more bad parts than good ones—in *Niagara* (a crazy film in which she played an idiot), *How to Marry a Millionaire* (briefly funny), *River of No Return* (riding a raft on a river with Robert Mitchum), There's *No Business Like Show Business* (a stinker), and *The Prince and the Showgirl* (a terrible humiliation). She was to go to London to make the film with Laurence Olivier. Again, she couldn't remember or focus. She couldn't play the long scenes. She was in awe of Olivier's reputation and helpless next to his great craft. When she wanted to know her character's motivation, he said, in despair. "Marilyn, just be sexy! Isn't that what you do?"

She had no answer to Olivier's question, and no way of saving face. She was with Arthur Miller now—about as different from Joe DiMaggio as anyone could be. They said they loved each other, and they were surrounded by reporters and photographers. Miller stood like a shy, gaunt tree, and Marilyn was the serpent writhing all over him, giving off the looks for the cameramen she knew so well. What that means is that she was so much more accustomed to photographers than he was—and so much more obedient to their nasty instincts. He believed in the inner life, and at thirty-two she had no map of the place.

Amid this chaos, and the fear that she was getting herself more and more drugged to get through crises, she made the two films that immortalize her. For Joshua Logan, she did *Bus Stop*, William Inge's play translated to the screen. It is a whole film for which she takes on a character and never allows herself one moment where

she winks and says, "Hi, it's me, Marilyn." Beautifully partnered by Don Murray, she does a superb rendering of a terrible version of "That Old Black Magic," easily the most skillful thing she ever put on film. And she is funny, tender, and moving. She is an actress.

Then there's Wilder's *Some Like It Hot*, in which she had the huge task of trying to divert attention from other "gals"—Jack Lemmon and Tony Curtis. It's a magnificent, daring film that was an ordeal to make. The boys were in tight, uncomfortable costumes, and Marilyn could never get anything right. The shooting went on and on. She needed sixty takes for one line: "It's me, Sugar." Curtis, for one, wondered if she was sabotaging the male comedy (which was usually good on three or four takes). Wilder cursed and persevered. She was the worst person to work with, he said, until you saw her face in dailies, and then the mixture of comedy and tragedy was extraordinary. He said she was as powerful as Garbo.

No one knew how little time she had left, though there were people close to her who worried about her loss of center. She was thirty-three in 1959, and she was on the point of a third divorce. She had no children (though there had been a miscarriage with Miller). Plenty of young women in America shared that career history, but something was happening to her famous looks. As a beach kid in California, she had worked out hard and kept in training. But now there was a weight problem, such as Judy Garland had suffered from. Booze and prescription drugs only added to it. But if you looked at her face you could see she was growing up. She was becoming a person. The merry, girlie look of 1950 was gone and now there was a woman of sorrows and experience. Great still photographers—Milton Greene, Bert Stern—saw this and capitalized on it.

The great virtue of a book like this is that it allows us to see the way in which Marilyn's romance with the still camera—with the moment—becomes clearer or more complete as her life went on. She understood that work so much better than playing in time and movement. In so many of her movies, she seems limited, naïve, someone being made fun of (whether she knows it or not). But in so many of the stills, she has an inner life, an array of moods, and a mounting sadness. It's as if she knows that no one can actually live for $1/50$ of a second at f.8, and then another. You have to put the stills or the moments together in sequence, in history, and with a sense of responsibility. But in those stills, she grows wiser, less lonely, and more serene. Norman Mailer made the astute observation that she began to look like a Kennedy. You can argue that it's because she was beginning to have a strange, perilous intimacy with some of them. But I think it's also because she saw and felt that this new young family was in tune with America in a way that Marilyn was. Just think, with a little more luck, Marilyn might have lived through the 1960s. She would have been only forty in 1966. She could have been the perfect older sister for the flower children.

Of course, like any great beauty, she would have been terrified at turning forty. The prevailing wisdom in Hollywood was that at that age, the world lost interest in you and switched to someone younger. In *How to Marry a Millionaire*, Marilyn (on the rise) had played with Betty Grable, thirty-seven and fading away, but the pinup goddess of the war years. Moreover, no one saw Marilyn as one of those business-like actresses who could take control of her career. Elizabeth Taylor, four years younger, got $1 million for *Cleopatra*, survived illness and scandal, and became a tough, enduring icon. On her last film project, *Something's Got to Give*, the one she was fired from, Marilyn had been getting only $100,000. We think of her now as one of the great stars, but in fact she never translated that into a substantial bank balance. Blame the studio system, with its reputation for crushing young talent? No, blame the actress, because by 1960 anyone as important as Monroe was supposed to have her own company, lawyers, defenses.

At the end, if she was not smart in the ways of powerful men, she could be forgiven for not knowing whether she was the fairy on top of the tree, or the tree itself. She had been sewn in to an amazing dress and pushed out into the spotlight to sing "Happy Birthday, Mr. President," so she was important. But she was also the pliant stooge in a guys' game where they could never own up to her. She had broken with Arthur Miller. There is an ugly story of a weekend, very close to her end, when she was Frank Sinatra's guest at his Cal-Neva lodge on Lake Tahoe and found herself being passed around like a bonus delicacy among show people and gangsters. And she didn't have the strength or the need to get up and walk away from it all,

because she still couldn't ignore what powerful men thought of her. She could believe she was finished. She could hardly remember which pills she had taken already.

And so, on August 5, 1962, she was found dead in a small house in Brentwood, California. In time, different versions of the story emerged. She was full of drugs, or empty. It hardly matters. She was naked on her bed—with just the air-conditioning on—in a sprawled pose such as she had been working on in the last few years. There were amazing photo-shoots, with Marilyn clutching a small sheet, and the cameraman on the lip of the bed, hardly knowing whether to get in with her or just keep pressing the button. It was her own romance—that a camera could have her. And now, all these years later, the camera gives back—she was a mother after all, because she had produced a family of images in the photographic emulsion that would provide generations of images long after her death. The sweetest, smartest, most knowing Marilyn is in the twilight of these great stills. She had found her place.

In death, she had few friends or supporters. DiMaggio was loyal to her for years—he never talked in public, but he tended her grave. Though she was close to broke, in her will she left whatever there was to Lee Strasberg, and in time that made the Strasberg family beneficiaries of about $8 million a year, the current income from the sale of her image.

For image had become empire. She would have been eighty in 2006. She was a movie star, but her power rests in the stills that were her raptures and her confessions.

1927 | Los Angeles, CA | Studio portrait of Norma Jeane Mortenson, born in 1926, at the age of 6 months. Her mother named her Norma after actress Norma Talmadge.

1928 | Los Angeles, CA | Norma Jeane, 2 years old.

March 1929 | Los Angeles, CA | Norma Jeane and her mother, Gladys Pearl Monroe Baker (both on the right), and two friends.

1929 | Los Angeles, CA | Portrait of Norma Jeane playing on the beach.

1930 | Los Angeles, CA | Young Norma Jeane (right) at the seaside.

1933 | Los Angeles, CA | Norma Jeane
at the age of 7.

"No one told me I was pretty when I was a little girl. All little girls should be told they're pretty, even if they aren't."

Marilyn Monroe

1938 | Los Angeles, CA | Norma Jeane accompanied by Ana Lower (seated behind her), with whom she lived as a teenager, and two unidentified women.

1941 | Norma Jeane (center), 15 years old, with friends.

1943 | Avalon, CA | Norma Jeane and Jim Dougherty, a neighbor and fellow student at the high school she attended, whom she married on June 19, 1942, at the age of 16.

June 1945 | Castle Rock State Park, CA

1943 | Norma Jeane applying makeup.

pages 20 and 21:

1946 | Los Angeles, CA | This was a pivotal year for Norma Jeane—after appearing on several magazine covers, she divorced her husband, Jim Dougherty, and signed an acting contract with Fox Studios under the name Marilyn Monroe, Marilyn after actress Marilyn Miller, and Monroe honoring her mother's maiden name.

"When I met her, she was a simple, eager young woman ... a decent-hearted kid whom Hollywood brought down, legs parted. She had a thin skin and a soul that hungered for acceptance by people she might look up to."

Elia Kazan

1950 | Los Angeles, CA | Marilyn
in Hollywood.

Left: Summer 1947 | Los Angeles, CA | Marilyn at the beach on skis for one of her first fashion photo shoots.

Opposite: August 13, 1949 | Marilyn on the cover of *Picture Post* magazine.

13 August, 1949

PICTURE POST

CLOUDLESS

HULTON'S NATIONAL WEEKLY

GERMANY TODAY
A Solemn Warning

4D

13 AUGUST, 1949

Vol. 44   No. 7

25

April 1947 | Hollywood, CA | Marilyn in her acting debut on the set of *Scudda Hoo ! Scudda Hay !* by F. Hugh Herbert (1948).

1947 | Marilyn posing for a photo op.

"I once asked why I had to wear a bathing suit for a toothpaste ad. He looked at me as if I was some kind of crazy!"

Marilyn Monroe

Opposite: 1949 | Hollywood, CA | Marilyn posed for photographer Tom Kelly for the calendar *Miss Golden Dreams* for the sum of $50. The United States Postal Service considered the photo pornographic and forbid its distribution in certain states. A retouched version appeared later with clothing drawn over the original photo. In December 1953, some of these photographs appeared in the first issue of *Playboy* magazine after Hugh Hefner, the editor, bought the negatives.

February 11, 1949 | Hollywood, CA | Marilyn executes an arabesque during a dance lesson.

June 1949 | New York, NY | Marilyn and actor Lon McCallister dining on the train taking them to Warrenburg, Missouri, to present the prize to the winner of a contest organized by *Dream Home* magazine. Marilyn was also promoting her latest film, *Love Happy*, directed by David Miller (1949). Monroe and McCallister had played together the previous year in *Scudda Hoo! Scudda Hay!*

ca. 1952 | Hollywood, CA | Portrait.

1951 | Marilyn during a poolside photo session.

"I knew how third-rate I was. I could actually feel my lack of talent, as if it were cheap clothes I was wearing inside. But, my God, how I wanted to learn, to change, to improve!"

Marilyn Monroe

1951 | Portrait of Marilyn wearing a bikini.

Left: September 11, 1951 | Hollywood, CA | Marilyn peruses the script of Fritz Lang's film *Clash by Night* (1952). The producer, Jerry Wald (also pictured), was considering casting her in it.

Opposite: 1952 | Under a five-year contract with 20th Century Fox signed in 1950, Marilyn poses in her little apartment for the lens of Philippe Halsman for *Life* magazine.

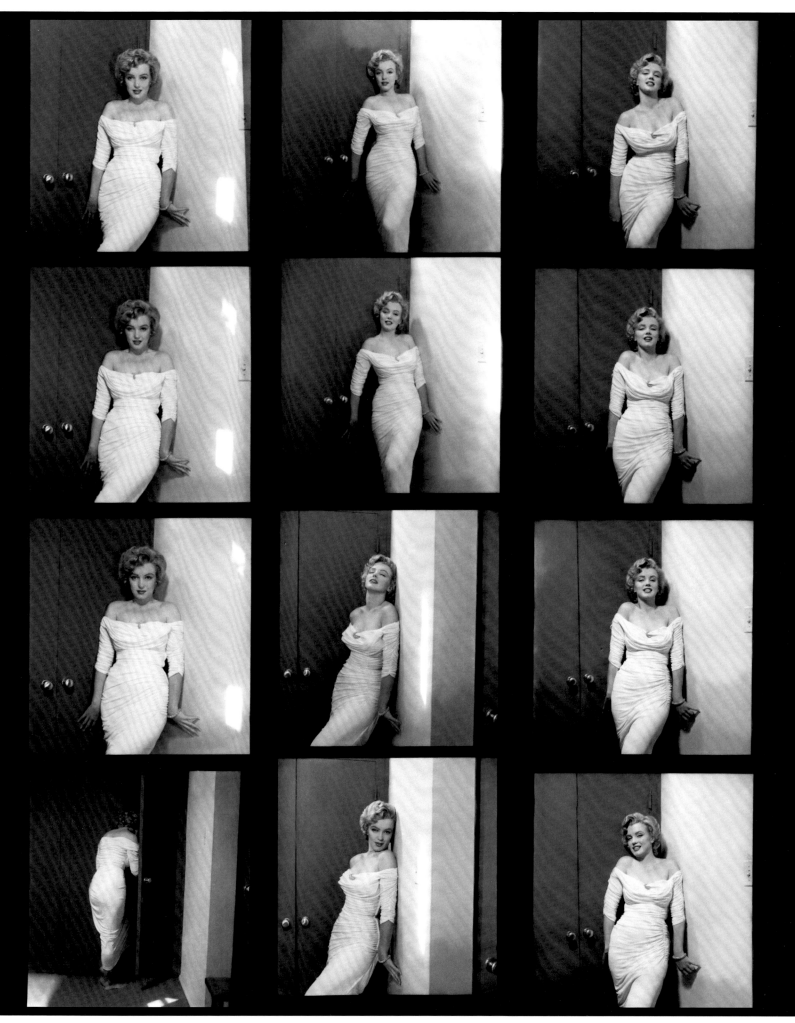

1952 | Marilyn portrait taken by
Philippe Halsman.

1951 | "Girl on a bearskin rug," studio photograph.

1957 | New York, NY | Marilyn at her
makeup table during a photo session.

1952 | Marilyn during a photo shoot for *Life* magazine.

"I found her marvelous to work with and terrifically ambitious to do better. And bright. She may not have had an education, but she was just naturally bright."

Henry Hathaway

1952 | Monterey, CA | Keith Andes and Marilyn in *Clash by Night* (1952).

May 1, 1953 | Hollywood, CA |
Marilyn at home.

1953 | Hollywood, CA | Marilyn on
the set of Henry Koster's film *Désirée*
(1954), featuring Marlon Brando.

"I just had to make it.
I was determined to
make it. Nothing was
going to get in my way."

Marilyn Monroe

ca. 1954 | Portrait of Marilyn.

1952 | Marilyn and Jane Russell
on the set of Howard Hawks' film
Gentlemen Prefer Blondes (1953).

1953 | Hollywood, CA | Marilyn surrounded by journalists as she leaves Grauman's Chinese Theatre, getting ready with Jane Russell to promote *Gentlemen Prefer Blondes*.

July 4, 1953 | Marilyn and a wardrobe mistress finish preparations for Marilyn's appearance during Fourth of July festivities celebrating America's independence.

July 2, 1953 | Marilyn poses for a
publicity shot – "Beware of Danger
July 4th."

"My work is the only ground I've ever had to stand on. I seem to have a whole superstructure with no foundation – but I'm working on the foundation." Marilyn Monroe

1952 | Hollywood, CA | Portrait.

1953 | Hollywood, CA | Marilyn at home, posing for the cover of *Life* magazine.

1955 | Marilyn posing at the beach in a bikini.

January 14, 1954 | San Francisco, CA |
Marilyn and baseball star Joe
DiMaggio share a kiss just
following their civil wedding.

56

1955 | New York, NY | Marilyn and Joe DiMaggio before the premiere of Billy Wilder's *The Seven Year Itch* (1955).

February 19, 1954 | Korea | Marilyn visiting and performing for American soldiers stationed in Korea.

February 26, 1954 | Korea | A heat wave unfolded over masses of American soldiers in Korea who gathered to hear Marilyn sing for them.

"I knew I belonged to the public and to the world, not because I was talented or even beautiful, but because I had never belonged to anything or anyone else."

Marilyn Monroe

February 26, 1954 | Korea | Marilyn signs an autograph during her visit to American soldiers stationed in Korea.

February 23, 1954 | Korea | Marilyn during her visit with American soldiers serving in Korea.

1954 | Palm Springs, CA | Marilyn at home.

pages 64 and 65:
1954 | Palm Springs, CA | Marilyn at her home.

1958 | New York, NY | Marilyn in her apartment at 444 East 57th Street.

1957 | Hollywood, CA | Marilyn with a 20th Century Fox executive.

pages 68 and 69:
1955 | Marilyn in relaxed moments.

"What she has – this presence, this luminosity, this flickering intelligence – could never surface on the stage .... It's like a hummingbird in flight. But anyone who thinks this girl is simply another Harlow or harlot or whatever is mad."

Constance Collier

1954 | Palm Springs, CA | Marilyn
at home.

November 1954 | Hollywood, CA | Marilyn learning to play "Chopsticks" with the assistance of Charles Smith, during the filming of Billy Wilder's *The Seven Year Itch* (1955).

September 1954 | New York, NY | Marilyn on the set of *The Seven Year Itch*.

November 1954 | Hollywood, CA | While waiting for the lighting to be adjusted on the set of *The Seven Year Itch*, Marilyn rehearses her lines one last time with her coach, Natasha Lytess.

November 1954 | Hollywood, CA | Marilyn leaving her dressing room in 20th Century Fox's on-locations studios during the filming of *The Seven Year Itch*.

1956 | New York, NY | Marilyn as seen through the lens of Elliott Erwitt.

1955 | New York, NY | Marilyn greets a group of teenagers on the set of *The Seven Year Itch*.

1954 | Hollywood, CA | With camera man Milton Krasner, Marilyn prepares to shoot a bathtub scene during the filming of *The Seven Year Itch*.

"The minute Marilyn hit the screen, everyone else was gone."

Richard Widmark

November 1954 | Hollywood, CA |
Marilyn taking a break between
filming scenes on the set of
The Seven Year Itch.

1954 | Hollywood, CA | At the studios of 20th Century Fox, Marilyn is interviewed by famous journalist Sidney Skolsky during the filming of *The Seven Year Itch*. As a result of this interview, Skolsky became Marilyn's friend, and wrote a book about her.

1955 | Marilyn at the premiere of Elia Kazan's *East of Eden*.

October 6, 1954 | Beverly Hills, CA | Marilyn bursts into tears in her lawyer Jerry Geisler's car following the announcement of the break up of her marriage with Joe DiMaggio after nine months of life together.

October 27, 1954 | New York, NY | Marilyn shields herself from photographers as she leaves the hospital.

1955 | New York, NY | Richard Avedon directs Marilyn during a photo session for *Vogue*.

1955 | New York, NY | Marilyn and Billy Wilder at a photo session at the studio of Richard Avedon, just before the New York premiere of *The Seven Year Itch*.

1956 | New York, NY | Marilyn signs autographs during the intermission of a Broadway show.

1955 | New York, NY | Marilyn and journalist Leonard Lyons in a fashionable cocktail lounge, the 21 Club, for an interview to appear in his column, "The Lyons Den," in *The New York Post*.

"Being a sex symbol is a heavy load to carry, especially when one is tired, hurt, and bewildered."

Marilyn Monroe

March 1955 | New York, NY | Portrait
at the Ambassador Hotel.

March 1955 | New York, NY |
In a subway station under Grand
Central Terminal, with director
Dick Shepherd.

March 1955 | New York, NY | Marilyn at the Ambassador Hotel, reading a book on acting techniques.

March 1955 | New York, NY |
Marilyn takes part in an
evening gala, the "Show of Shows,"
at Madison Square Garden, a benefit
for the fight against arthritis and
rheumatism. At the close of the
evening, she announced the creation,
with Milton Greene, of Marilyn
Monroe Productions.

1955 | New York, NY | Marilyn in the bedroom of her apartment on 444 East 57th Street.

March 1955 | New York, NY | Marilyn
applies Chanel No. 5 perfume at the
Ambassador Hotel.

1955 | Long Island, NY

"I want to grow old without facelifts. I want to have the courage to be loyal to the face I have made."

Marilyn Monroe

1955 | Bement, IL | Marilyn meets the oldest woman living in the small town of Bement, Illinois.

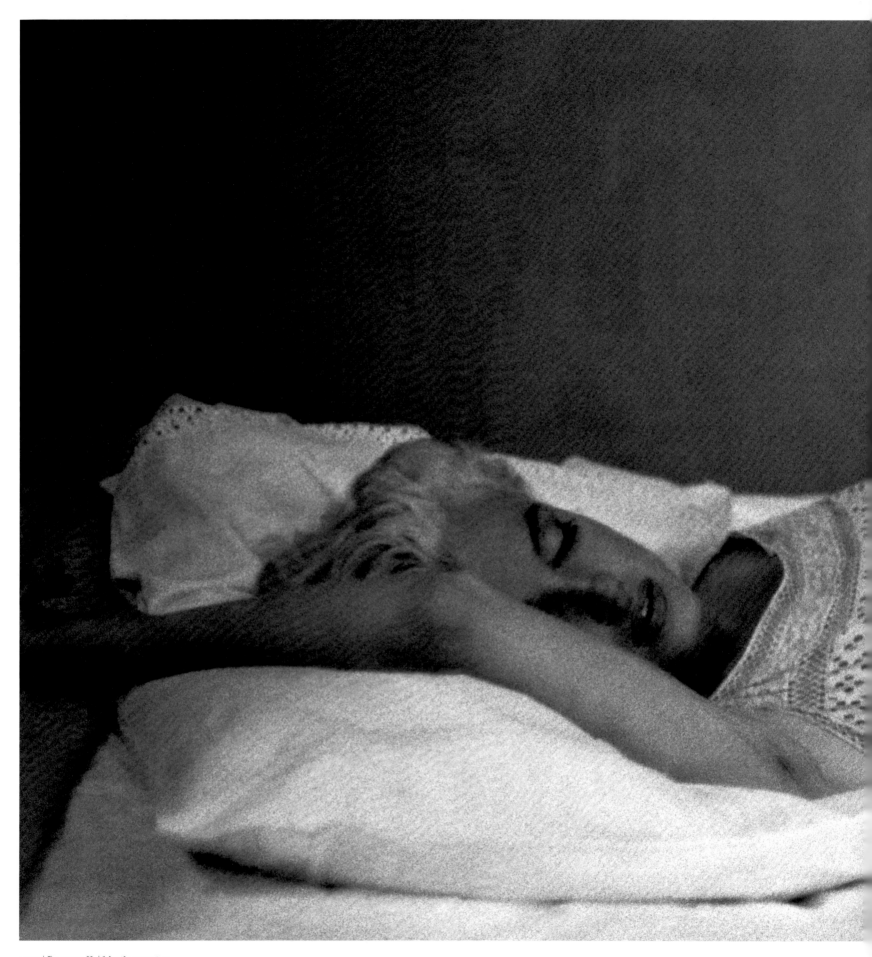

1955 | Bement, IL | Marilyn resting.

"Somehow, I don't think she'll make old bones. Absurd of me to say, but somehow I feel she'll go young. . . . I hope, I really pray, that she survives long enough to free the strange, lovely talent that's wandering through her like a jailed spirit."

Constance Collier

1955 | Illinois | Marilyn en route to Bement.

1955 | Amagansett, NY

March 1955 | New York, NY | Marilyn smoking a cigarette in a bar.

1955 | Los Angeles, CA | Marilyn leaving her dressing room during the shooting of Josh Logan's film *Bus Stop* (1956).

1955 | Los Angeles, CA | Don Murray and Marilyn smile for the camera while playing a scene that includes a kiss in *Bus Stop*.

1955 | Marilyn on the set of the film *Bus Stop*.

1956 | New York, NY | Marilyn and
John Huston.

February 25, 1956 | Los Angeles, CA | Marilyn and photographer Milton Greene arriving from New York at the Los Angeles airport.

June 2, 1956 | New York, NY | Marilyn arrives at Idlewild Airport on her return from the West Coast. She had just celebrated her 30th birthday.

pages 112 and 113:
February 1956 | New York, NY | Marilyn and director Laurence Olivier hold a press conference at the Waldorf-Astoria Hotel to announce the beginning of filming for *The Prince and the Showgirl* (1957), the first creation of Marilyn Monroe Productions.

"I was talking to Olivier one night . . . and he was saying it was a miracle to get her to do anything. But then he said, 'I finish the day and I go to look at the rushes, and she's batted me right off the screen.' That's Marilyn."

Richard Widmark

February, 1956 | New York, NY | Marilyn with Laurence Olivier at the press conference at the Waldorf-Astoria Hotel for *The Prince and the Showgirl* (1957).

June 21, 1956 | New York, NY | Marilyn poses as she leaves her Sutton Place apartment. Arthur Miller, having testified before the House Un-American Activities Committee, had just announced that they would be married.

June 29, 1956 | Roxbury, CT | Arthur Miller kisses Marilyn's forehead during a press conference at his home. That same evening they were married in White Plains, New York.

1956 | New York, NY | Marilyn and
Arthur Miller on Harlem River Drive,
in front of the Queensboro Bridge

1956 | New York, NY | Marilyn and Arthur Miller in Battery Park.

1956 | New York, NY | Marilyn and
Arthur Miller in his Ford Thunderbird
on Harlem River Drive.

September 1956 | New York, NY | Marilyn in Central Park during a shoot for an article on "A day in Marilyn's life" for *Look* magazine.

"I could've looked down my nose at you, too—just a kid showin' herself off in nightclubs for so much a night. But I took my hat off to you. Because I know the difference."

The character Gay Langland in *The Misfits*, by Arthur Miller

Summer 1957 | Amagansett, NY | Marilyn and Arthur Miller sharing a day at the beach.

1957 | Amagansett, NY | Marilyn jumping for joy on the beach at Amagansett, Long Island.

Summer 1957 | Amagansett, NY |
Marilyn and Arthur Miller.

June 1957 | Amagansett, NY | Marilyn and Arthur Miller enjoying the beach at Amagansett.

July 1956 | London, England | Marilyn arrives at Heathrow airport in London, accompanied by her husband, Arthur Miller.

1956 | Englefield Green, England | Marilyn photographed at the house she stayed at while filming *The Prince and the Showgirl*.

1957 | Marilyn in *The Prince and the Showgirl*.

1957 | New York, NY | Marilyn seated beside her husband during a party for the premiere of *The Prince and the Showgirl*. On her right is the mayor of New York, Robert F. Wagner, Jr.

1957 | New York, NY | Marilyn at Radio City Music Hall during the premiere of *The Prince and the Showgirl*.

"There is something exceptionally lively and alert about her, an intelligence. It's her character, a look, something very subtle, very lively, that disappears quickly in order to reappear anew."

Henri Cartier-Bresson

1958 | Roxbury, CT | Marilyn on
Arthur Miller's property.

May 22, 1958 | New York, NY |
Producer Kermit Bloomingdale visits
Arthur Miller and Marilyn at their
home in New York.

1957 | Amagansett, NY | In a cottage rented for the summer, as so often, Marilyn is on the phone.

137

1957 | Roxbury, CT | Marilyn and her basset hound, Hugo, on the grounds of Arthur Miller's estate.

August 10, 1957 | New York, NY | Arthur Miller looks after Marilyn as she leaves the hospital after spending 10 days there following a miscarriage.

"... if there could be one person in the world ... a child who could be brave from the beginning ..."

The character Roslyn Taber in *The Misfits*, by Arthur Miller

September 1954 | New York, NY | Marilyn on the set of Billy Wilder's *The Seven Year Itch* (1955). She wrote along the edge of this photo, "This is my favorite."

1959 | Marilyn and Tony Curtis at an event promoting the Billy Wilder film *Some Like It Hot* (1959).

1959 | Marilyn on the set of *Some Like It Hot* with one of her male co-stars, Tony Curtis.

1958 | Roxbury, CT | Marilyn and
Arthur Miller.

1958 | Roxbury, CT | Marilyn during a photo session.

"Her beauty and humanity shine through . . . she is the kind of artist one does not come upon every day in the week. After all, she was created something extraordinary."

Arthur Miller

Summer 1958 | Roxbury, CT | Marilyn photographed at the home of her husband, Arthur Miller.

1959 | Brooklyn, NY | In New York for the release of the film *Some Like It Hot*, Marilyn takes a side trip to Ebbets Field baseball stadium .

February 5, 1959 | Nyack, NY | Marilyn and Arthur Miller attend a dinner organized by writer Carson McCullers (kissing Marilyn) in honor of celebrated Danish author Isak Dinesen (at the head of the table), also known by her original name, Baroness Karen Blixen.

"She has a certain indefinable magic that comes across, which no other actress in the business has."

Billy Wilder

1960 | Hollywood, CA | During the shooting of John Huston's *The Misfits* (1961).

"When you look at Marilyn on the screen, you don't want anything bad to happen to her. You really care that she should be all right . . . happy."

Natalie Wood

1959 | With Yves Montand on the set of George Cukor's *Let's Make Love* (1960).

1960 | Los Angeles, CA | Marilyn during a recording session in a Hollywood studio.

1960 | Nevada | Marilyn as captured on film by Ernst Haas.

1960 | Nevada | Marilyn during the filming of *The Misfits*.

1960 | Nevada | Marilyn and Eli Wallach are directed by John Huston during the filming of *The Misfits*.

1960 | Nevada | Marilyn's makeup is touched up on the set of *The Misfits*.

1960 | Reno, NV | Marilyn spending an evening at a casino in Reno with director John Huston, near the filming location of *The Misfits*. Huston sometimes spent entire nights in the casino, and Marilyn decided to accompany him since the filming was almost finished.

"Everything Marilyn does is different from any other woman, strange and exciting, from the way she talks to the way she uses that magnificent torso."

Clark Gable

1960 | Nevada | Marilyn and Eli
Wallach on the set of *The Misfits*.

pages 164 and 165: 1960 | Nevada | Marilyn and Arthur Miller on the set of *The Misfits*, during the course of which they separated.

"Nobody discovered her, she earned her own way to stardom."

Darryl Zanuck

1960 | Nevada | Marilyn on the set of *The Misfits*.

1960 | Hollywood, CA | Marilyn watching the rushes of *The Misfits*.

November 1960 | New York, NY | Marilyn is assailed by the press as she leaves her home after the announcement of her separation from Arthur Miller.

"Dogs never bite me. Just humans."

Marilyn Monroe

March 1961 | Marilyn during a gala dinner.

1961 | Hollywood, CA | A photo session with photographer Douglas Kirkland.

1961 | Hollywood, CA | Marilyn as photographed by Douglas Kirkland.

"Even though I was born there, I still can't think of one good thing to say about it. If I close my eyes, and picture L.A., all I see is one big varicose vein."

Marilyn Monroe

April 2, 1961 | New York, NY

1961 | New York, NY | Marilyn and
Joe DiMaggio attending a baseball
game at Yankee Stadium.

July 11, 1961 | New York, NY | Marilyn leaves the hospital after having her gall bladder removed.

1961 | Marilyn in the hands of the famous hairdresser to the stars, Kenneth Battelle. Battelle is best known as the creator of Jackie Kennedy's chic hairstyle.

1962 | Marilyn in rehearsal with her coach, Paula Strasberg, wife of Lee Strasberg, founder of the renowned Actors Studio in New York where Marilyn studied. Marilyn had complete confidence in Paula, even when it meant contradicting the instructions of directors with whom she was working.

pages 180 and 181:

May 29, 1962 | Washington, DC | Marilyn purrs "Happy Birthday, Mr President" during a party celebrating President John F. Kennedy's 45th birthday. That evening, she gave him an inscribed gold Rolex watch, along with a poem entitled "A Heartfelt Plea on Your Birthday": " Let lovers breathe their sighs/And roses bloom and music sound/ Let passion burn on lips and eyes/ And pleasure's merry world go round/ Let golden sunshine flood the sky/ And let me love/ Or let me die!" When JFK received this gift from the hands of his aide Kenneth O'Donnell, he is said to have quipped to O'Donnell "Get rid of it!"

"When I think of the future, I think, I'm thirty-six years old. I am just getting started."

Marilyn Monroe

1961 | Marilyn on the set of *Something's Got To Give*, directed by George Cukor (1962). This photo is a still taken directly from the rushes, as the film was never completed.

1962 | Los Angeles, CA | Photographer Bert Stern managed to arrange two photo sessions with Marilyn, for *Vogue* magazine. In one session she was nude, too nude for *Vogue*. In the other she wore more clothing and makeup. In those two sessions, 2,571 shots were taken. Marilyn died the day before photographs from those shoots appeared in *Vogue*.

June 1962 | Los Angeles, CA | One of the last photographs of Marilyn. It was taken by her friend George Barris and was intended to be included in an autobiographical book responding to 20th Century Fox's suspension of the actress.

August 5, 1962 | Los Angeles, CA |
Death of Marilyn Monroe.

August 13, 1962 | Hollywood, CA | Joe DiMaggio brushes away tears as he leaves Marilyn's funeral at Westwood Memorial Park.

"Marilyn! Marilyn! Why did everything have to turn out the way it did? Why does life have to be so fucking rotten?"

Music for Chameleons, Truman Capote

Opposite:
Summer 1958 | Roxbury, CT | Snapshot of Marilyn at Arthur Miller's home in Connecticut.

188

TIMELINE

June 1, 1926	Norma Jeane Mortenson born at Los Angeles General Hospital
1935	Norma Jeane's mother, Gladys Baker (born Monroe), is placed in an institution
September 13, 1935	Norma Jeane enters an orphanage in Los Angeles as orphan no. 3463
June 26, 1937	Norma Jeane leaves the orphanage to live with Grace McKee
November 1938	Norma Jeane goes to live with "Aunt" Ana Lower
June 19, 1942	Norma Jeane marries Jim Dougherty
April 1944	Norma Jeane starts working at the Radio Plane Munitions Factory
1946	First photo shoots as a model
August 26, 1946	First studio contract with 20th Century Fox. Norma Jeane changes her name to Marilyn Monroe
September 16, 1946	Divorce from Jim Dougherty
1947	First minor appearances in feature films
August 25, 1947	Marilyn's Fox contract is not renewed
March 9, 1948	Marilyn signs a contract with Columbia Pictures
September 8, 1948	Marilyn's Columbia Pictures contract is not renewed
May 27, 1949	Poses naked for photographer Tom Kelley
August 15, 1949	Filming of A Ticket To Tomahawk begins
October 1949	Signs contract with MGM for role in The Asphalt Jungle
January 5, 1950	Filming of The Fireball begins
April 1950	Marilyn plays a small part in All About Eve
December 10, 1950	Signs a new contract with 20th Century Fox
April 18, 1951	Filming of Love Nest begins
May 11, 1951	Marilyn's contract with 20th Century Fox is converted to a seven-year deal
September 8, 1951	First full-length feature of Marilyn in Collier's magazine
March 1952	Marilyn and baseball star Joe DiMaggio go out on their first date
April 7, 1952	First Life magazine cover
August 31, 1952	First live radio interview
January 21, 1953	Niagara is released, Marilyn experiences stardom
September 13, 1953	Marilyn's first television appearance, on The Jack Benny Show
October 1953	Meets Milton Greene at a party given by Gene Kelly
November 4, 1953	How to Marry a Millionaire premieres
December 1953	Marilyn fails to appear on the first day of filming of The Girl in the Pink Tights
January 4, 1954	20th Century Fox suspends Marilyn
January 14, 1954	Marilyn and Joe DiMaggio marry at San Francisco City Hall
February 16, 1954	Marilyn starts ten-venue tour for U.S. troops in Korea
October 27, 1954	Officially separates from Joe DiMaggio
December 31, 1954	Marilyn and Milton Greene form Marilyn Monroe Productions
February 1955	Marilyn meets and begins studying acting with Lee Strasberg
March 31, 1955	Rides a pink elephant at Madison Square Garden for arthritis benefit
June 1, 1955	The Seven Year Itch premieres
October 31, 1955	Granted official divorce from Joe DiMaggio
February 25, 1956	Returns to Hollywood after more than one year away in New York
May 3, 1956	Bus Stop filming begins
June 3, 1956	Marilyn returns to New York after finishing work on Bus Stop
June 29 / July 1, 1956	Marries playwright Arthur Miller
July 14, 1956	Arrives in London to begin work with Laurence Olivier in The Prince and The Showgirl
August 1956	Marilyn becomes pregnant but has a miscarriage
October 29, 1956	Presented to Queen Elizabeth II at the royal command film performance
June 13, 1957	The Prince and the Showgirl premieres
August 1, 1957	Ectopic pregnancy has to be terminated
August 4, 1958	Starts work on Some Like it Hot
December 17, 1958	Suffers another miscarriage
March 29, 1959	Premiere of Some Like it Hot
March 8, 1960	Receives Golden Globe Award (Best Comedy Actress) for her role in Some Like it Hot
June 1960	Begins seeing psychoanalyst Ralph Greenson on a daily basis
July 18, 1960	Filming of The Misfits begins
August 26, 1960	Flies to Los Angeles because of nervous breakdown during filming
November 11, 1960	Public announcement that Marilyn and Arthur Miller are to divorce
January 31, 1961	Premiere of The Misfits
February 7, 1961	Marilyn enters Payne Whitney Psychiatric Clinic in New York
February 11, 1961	Joe DiMaggio arranges for Marilyn to be transferred to the less intimidating Columbia Presbyterian Hospital
March 5, 1961	Discharged from Columbia Presbyterian Hospital
October 1961	Marilyn meets Robert F. Kennedy at Peter Lawford's beach house
November 19, 1961	Attends a dinner at Peter Lawford's house with President Kennedy
February 1962	Moves into a house she has bought in Brentwood, Los Angeles
March 5, 1962	Marilyn wins Golden Globe Award (World's Film Favorite)
March 24, 1962	Marilyn and JFK spend the weekend together in Palm Springs
April 23, 1962	Work begins on Something's Got to Give
May 19, 1962	Sings "Happy Birthday" and "Thanks for the Memory" to JFK at Madison Square Garden
June 7, 1962	20th Century Fox fires Marilyn for breach of contract
June 23, 1962	Bert Stern begins first of three photo sessions for Vogue magazine
June 29, 1962	George Barris does a 3-day photo shoot of Marilyn for Cosmopolitan
July 4, 1962	Begins extensive interview with Richard Meryman
July 6, 1962	Allan Grant photo session for Life magazine
July 12, 1962	Meets 20th Century Fox studio chiefs regarding difficulties during the filming of Something's Got to Give
July 20, 1962	Enters hospital for abortion
August 1, 1962	20th Century Fox rewrites Marilyn's contract for double the salary and restarts production of Something's Got to Give
August 3, 1962	Marilyn appears on the cover of Life magazine
August 5, 1962	Police called to Marilyn's home. Official day of death. Autopsy performed
August 8, 1962	Funeral at Westwood Medical Park Cemetery

PHOTO CREDITS

10 | Hulton Archive / Getty Images
11 | Archive Photos / Getty Images
11–17 | Silver Screen / Getty Images
18 | William Carroll / Corbis
19 | Silver Screen / Getty Images
20 | Movie Star / Superstock / Sipa
21 | Sipa
23 | Sunset Boulevard / Corbis
24 | Silver Screen / Getty Images
25 | André de Dienes / Picture Post / Getty Images
26 | Bettmann / Corbis
27 | Frank Driggs / Rue des Archives
29 | Coll-Movie Star / Superstock / Sipa
30 | J.R. Eyerman / Time Life Pictures / Getty Images
31 | Hulton Archive / Getty Images
32 | Underwood & Underwood / Corbis
33 & 35 | Hulton Archive / Getty Images
36 | Bob Landry / Time Life Pictures / Getty Images
37 & 38 | Philippe Halsman / Magnum Photos
39 | Hulton Archive / Getty Images
40 | Sam Shaw / Roger-Viollet
41 | Philippe Halsman / Magnum Photos
43 | John Springer Collection / Corbis
44 | Alfred Eisenstaedt / Time Life Pictures / Getty Images
45 | Dennis Stock / Magnum Photos
47 | Pele Coll / Stills / Gamma
48 | Ed Clark / Time Life Pictures / Getty Images
49 | Murray Garrett / Getty Images
50–51 | Bettmann / Corbis
53 | Hulton-Deutsch Collection / Corbis
54 | Alfred Eisenstaedt / Time Life Pictures / Getty Images
55 | CinemaPhoto / Corbis
56 | Bettmann / Corbis
57 | Sam Shaw / Roger-Viollet
58–59 | Bettmann / Corbis
61 | Mai / Time Life Pictures / Getty Images

62 | Bettmann / Corbis
63–65 | ST Nahum Baron / Getty Images
66–67 | Sam Shaw / Roger-Viollet
68–69 | Hulton Archive / Getty Images
71 | ST Nahum Baron / Getty Images
72–75 | Sam Shaw / Roger-Viollet
76 | Elliott Erwitt / Magnum Photos
78 | Eve Arnold / Magnum Photos
79–82 | Sam Shaw / Roger-Viollet
83 | Eve Arnold / Magnum Photos
84–85 | Bettmann / Corbis
86–89 | Sam Shaw / Roger-Viollet
91–93 | Michael Ochs Archives / Corbis
94 | Milton Greene Archives / AFP
95 | Sam Shaw / Roger-Viollet
96 | Michael Ochs Archives / Corbis
97–104 | Eve Arnold / Magnum Photos
105 | Michael Ochs Archives / Corbis
106 | Dennis Stock / Magnum Photos
107 | Gene Lester / Getty Images
108 | Dennis Stock / Magnum Photos
109 | Burt Glinn / Magnum Photos
110 | Hulton Archive / Getty Images
111 | Bettmann / Corbis
112 | Michael Ochs Archives / Corbis
113–115 | Eve Arnold / Magnum Photos
116–117 | Bettmann / Corbis
118–127 | Sam Shaw / Roger-Viollet
128 | AFP
129 | Hulton-Deutsch Collection / Corbis
130 | Pele Coll / Stills / Gamma
131 | Sam Shaw / Roger-Viollet
132 | Larry Shaw / Roger-Viollet
135 | Sam Shaw / Roger-Viollet
136 | Robert W. Kelley / Time Life Pictures / Getty Images
137–138 | Sam Shaw / Roger-Viollet

139 | Associated Press / Sipa Press
141 | Sam Shaw / Roger-Viollet
142 | John Kobal Foundation / Getty Images
143 | Pele Coll / Stills / Gamma
144–147 | Sam Shaw / Roger-Viollet
148 | Bob Henriques / Magnum Photos
149 | Bettmann / Corbis
151 | Philippe Halsman / Magnum Photos
152–153 | Bruce Davidson / Magnum Photos
155 | John Bryson / Time Life Pictures / Getty Images
156 | Bruce Davidson / Magnum Photos
157–159 | Ernst Haas / Getty Images
160 | Bruce Davidson / Magnum Photos
161 | Eve Arnold / Magnum Photos
163 | Inge Morath / Magnum Photos
164 | Ernst Haas / Getty Images
165 | Bruce Davidson / Magnum Photos
167 | Inge Morath / Magnum Photos
168 | Elliott Erwitt / Magnum Photos
169 | Hulton Archive / Getty Images
171 | Europresse / Sygma / Corbis
172–173 | Douglas Kirkland / Corbis
175 | Bettmann / Corbis
176 | Lee Lockwood / Time Life Pictures / Getty Images
177 | Bettmann / Corbis
178 | Eve Arnold / Magnum Photos
179 | Lawrence Schiller & William Read Woodfield / Gamma
180 | Associated Press / Sipa Press
181 | Cecil B. Stoughton / JFK Library
183 | Scope / Stills / Gamma / Hachette Filipacchi Photos
184 | AP Photo / Brooklyn Museum of Art, Bert Stern / Sipa Press
185 | George Barris
187 | Keystone / Getty Images
189 | Sam Shaw / Roger-Violle

ACKNOWLEDGMENTS

"A vous deux que j'aime. Pour votre présence, votre constance et votre lumière."
"To the two I love. For your presence, your constancy, and your light."

Anne Verlhac

The editor would like to thank the following people, in alphabetical order:

Hervé Autran, Michèle Riesenmey, Larry Shaw, Michael Shulman, Steve Spelman, and David Thomson.

First published in the United States in 2007 by Chronicle Books LLC.
First published in France in 2007 by Verlhac Éditions.

ISBN-10: 0-8118-6147-3
ISBN-13: 978-0-8118-6147-2

Manufactured in Italy.

Translated and typeset by Anne Slater and Tammi Reichel for APE Int'l

Distributed in Canada by Raincoast Books
9050 Shaughnessy Street
Vancouver, British Columbia V6P 6E5

10 9 8 7 6 5 4 3 2 1

Chronicle Books LLC
680 Second Street
San Francisco, California 94107

www.chroniclebooks.com